CU00952123

MATHS & ENGLISH FOR
HOSPITALITY AND CATERING

Graduated exercises and practice exam

Andrew Spencer and Neil Rippington

CENGAGE
Learning®

Australia • Brazil • Japan • Korea • Mexico • Singapore • Spain • United Kingdom • United States

Maths & English for Hospitality and Catering

Andrew Spencer and Neil Rippington

Publishing Director: Linden Harris

Commissioning Editor: Lucy Mills

Development Editor: Claire Napoli

Production Editor: Alison Cooke

Production Controller: Eyvett Davis

Marketing Manager: Lauren Mottram

Typesetter: Cenveo Publisher Services

Cover design: HCT Creative

For product information and technology assistance, contact **emea.info@cengage.com**.

For permission to use material from this text or product, and for permission queries, email **emea.permissions@cengage.com**.

This work is Adapted from Pre Apprenticeship: Maths & Literacy Series by Andrew Spencer, published by Cengage Learning Australia Pty Limited © 2010.

British Library Cataloguing-in-Publication Data
A catalogue record for this book is available from the British Library.

ISBN: 978-1-4080-7269-1

Cengage Learning EMEA
Cheriton House, North Way, Andover, Hampshire, SP10 5BE, United Kingdom

Cengage Learning products are represented in Canada by Nelson Education Ltd.

For your lifelong learning solutions, visit
www.cengage.co.uk

Purchase your next print book, e-book or e-chapter at
www.cengagebrain.com

Printed in Malta by Melita Press
1 2 3 4 5 6 7 8 9 10 – 14 13 12

Maths & English for Hospitality and Catering

Contents

Introduction

It has always been important to understand, from a teacher's perspective, the nature of the maths skills students need for their future, rather than teaching them textbook mathematics. This has been a guiding principle behind the development of the content in this workbook. To teach maths and English that is *relevant* to students seeking apprenticeships is the best that we can do, to give students an education in the field they would like to work in.

The content in this resource is aimed at the level that is needed for a student to have the best possibility of improving their mathematical and English skills specifically for Hospitality and Catering. Students can use this workbook to prepare for their functional skills assessment, or to even assist with basic maths and English for their Hospitality and Catering qualification. This resource has the potential to improve students' understanding of basic mathematical concepts that can be applied to the Hospitality industry and a Catering environment. These resources have been trialled, and they work.

Commonly used industry terms are introduced so that students have a basic understanding of terminology they will encounter in the workplace environment. Students who can complete this workbook and reach a higher outcome in all topics will have achieved the goal of this resource.

The content in this workbook is the first step to bridging the gap between what has been learned in previous years, and what needs to be remembered and re-learned for use in exams and in the workplace. Students will significantly benefit from the consolidation of the basic maths and English concepts.

In many ways, it is a 'win-win situation', with students enjoying and studying relevant maths and English for work and training organizations and employers receiving students that have improved basic maths and English skills.

All that is needed is patience, hard work, a positive attitude, a belief in yourself that you can do it and a desire to achieve. The rest is up to you.

About the authors

Andrew Spencer has studied education both within Australia and overseas. He has a Bachelor of Education, as well as a Masters of Science in which he specialized in teacher education. Andrew has extensive experience in teaching secondary mathematics throughout New South Wales and South Australia for well over 15 years. He has taught a range of subject areas, including Maths, English, Science, Classics, Physical Education and Technical Studies. His sense of the importance of practical mathematics has continued to develop with the range of subject areas he has taught in.

Neil Rippington has adapted Maths and English for Hospitality and Catering. Neil is Dean of the College of Food at University College Birmingham. He has 20 years experience in hospitality education as a Chef Lecturer, Quality Manager, Curriculum Manager and Head of Department. He has a Bachelor of Arts Degree in Education and Training and a Masters Degree in Culinary Arts. He has taught a range of subjects including Professional Cookery, Hospitality Management as well as Maths and English in Hospitality and Catering.

Acknowledgements

Andrew Spencer:
For Paula, Zach, Katelyn, Mum and Dad.
  Many thanks to Mal Aubrey (GTA) and all training organizations for their input.
  To the De La Salle Brothers for their selfless work with all students.
  Thanks also to Dr Pauline Carter for her unwavering support of all maths teachers.
  This is for all students who value learning, who are willing to work hard and who have character … and are characters!

Neil Rippington:
Amanda, my wife, for her continued and highly valued support. Joseph, Luke and Freya, my children, for making sure that every day is a unique one.

Unit 1: Spelling

Short-answer questions

Specific instructions to students

- This is an exercise to help you identify and to correct spelling errors.
- Read the activity below, then answer accordingly.

Read the following passage and identify and correct the spelling errors.

A kitchen at a Asian and Oriental restarant is praparing the dinner menu. The chef knows it will be a busy night as they have over 300 people booked in for dinner. The chef checks the menu and finds that there needs to be some chainges. A veal dish is taken off and repluced with a Thai chillie beef. A Goan fish curry is also added to the menu along with a chucken and cashew stir-friy. The chef asks the sous chef to beggin preparation of starters, which include roasted pupper and sundraid tomatto Pâté; pumkin and cummin dips; savoury bread cases and seefood frittars. The sous chef is assisted by a commis chef who helps out regularly with the food preperation.

The chef also starts to prepare some of the main courses. These include chicken jalousie; chicken Charlotte; Italian tomato caserole; pork and vegetuble cury; beef vindaloo; chilli sesamee prawn kebabes and olive and lemmon lamb catlets. It is getting closer to opening time and everyone is busey completing the preparation of the food. Meanwhile, at the front of the restarant, the manger sets some tasks for the too waiters. The tables need to be prepared for the guests and all the tables need seting. The cutlery needs to be checked and set in the apropriate order.

Incorrect words:

_____

_____

_____

Correct words:

_____

_____

_____

Unit 2: Alphabetizing

Short-answer questions

Specific instructions to students

- In this unit, you will be able to practise your alphabetizing skills.
- Read the activity below, then answer accordingly.

Put the following words into alphabetical order.

Cutlery	Hot plate
Commis chef	Oven
Table setting	Ladle
Cooking	Restaurant
Barista	Defrosted
Waiter	Extra virgin olive oil
Manager	Whisk

Answer:

Unit 3: Comprehension

Short-answer questions

Specific instructions to students

- This is an exercise to help you understand what you read.
- Read the following activity, then answer the questions that follow.

Read the following passage and answer the questions in sentence form.

The wedding attracted a congregation of 180 guests and the bride arrived at 12.45 p.m. She was supposed to arrive at 12.15 p.m., but as tradition goes, she was suitably late. The ceremony was conducted by a registrar in the beautiful southern parklands. Everyone was looking forward to the reception at the Regal Hotel, which was only a few kilometres away. Everyone that is, except the head chef. Two staff members who were scheduled to work were away sick with influenza, and only one was able to be replaced prior to the guests arriving. The tables had been set by the two waiters and the manager had the function room ready for the reception.

As the guests were seated, the waiters moved around the room, taking orders for the main course. The guests could choose between chicken or fish. 123 guests ordered the chicken, while everyone else ordered the fish. The head chef immediately started cooking but there was one problem … the suppliers only delivered 110 portions of chicken and 110 portions of fish. 200 guests were expected but several did not attend for various reasons. What could the chef do? The starters had been sent and many of the guests were waiting for their main course. The waiters quickly shuffled between the tables, asking guests if they could have fish instead of chicken. Most agreed, but a few guests began to get angry that they couldn't have the chicken. The manager did a great job calming down those who were inconvenienced, by apologizing and offering a free bottle of wine to each guest to help quell their anger. This gesture was met with immediate success – all guests relaxed and enjoyed their meal and the wine!

QUESTION 1

How late was the bride for the wedding ceremony?

Answer:

QUESTION 2

What was the first major problem that the head chef faced?

Answer:

QUESTION 3

Who prepared the tables at the front of the hotel for the reception?

Answer:

QUESTION 4

How many guests ordered the chicken?

Answer:

QUESTION 5

How many guests ordered the fish?

Answer:

QUESTION 6

How did the manager deal with the angry guests?

Answer:

Unit 4: Grammar

Section A: Apostrophes

Using apostrophes is simple when you know how. You need to follow some basic rules.

The two main reasons for using apostrophes are as follows:

1. To show a letter, or letters, is left out in a word or letters that are left out when two words are joined.

2. To show possession (something belongs to someone or a group. This can be a tangible (physical/touchable/ material) item, such as a mobile phone, or something that is not, such as an emotion or an opinion).

Short-answer questions

Using the first rule, complete the following sentences.

The first use of an apostrophe is to show where a letter, or letters, has been missed out

'Do not' is reduced to 'don't'.	The apostrophe is placed where the letter 'o' in 'not' has been left out.

EXAMPLE

I don't (do not) have to go to work tonight.

1. (We are) _____booked in at eight o'clock .

2. (It is) _____ great to see you again.

3. (They are) _____ very good at their job.

4. It (is not) _____ fair to make him clean the kitchen on his own.

5. (I am) _____ thinking of applying for a new job.

6. (It is)_____the first time I've eaten sushi.

7. (What is) _____ your favourite dessert?

8. (It is) _____a very nice wine and (I am) _____ sure (they will) _____ enjoy it.

9. (You are)_____not scheduled to work tomorrow?

10. (It will) _____ be worth it when (you have)_____ finished.

The 2nd use of an apostrophe to show someone, or something, possesses (owns) something.

1. Owned or in the possession of one person or thing.

EXAMPLE

Simon (owns a book)   Simon's book

2. Owned or in the possession of a group of people, or things. For example:

(for plural words ending in the letter 's'.)

EXAMPLE

Ladies (have a changing room)   Ladies' changing room

(for plural words that do not end with the letter 's', e.g., team, children)

EXAMPLE

Men (belong to an association)   Men's association

There is one exception to the rules above. When a name finishes with the letter 's', e.g. Jones, Wilkins, Thomas, it is not necessary to add another 's' after the apostrophe. However, it is also not incorrect to add an extra 's'.

EXAMPLE

Mr Wilkins (owns a credit card)   Mr Wilkins' credit card (or) Mr Wilkins's credit card

Both are acceptable!

Exercise 2

Short-answer questions

Place the apostrophe in the correct place in the following examples. Consider who, or what, is the owner (in possession) and if it is plural or singular.

1. A waiter owns a bottle opener

   _____

2. A chef owns a knife

   _____

3. Neighbours have an extension

   _____

4. Members belong to a club

   _____

5. The team split their tips

   _____

6. A couple have a voucher for a free meal

   _____

7. A customer has a complaint

   _____

8. The oven has a thermometer

   _____

9. An alliance owned by chefs

   _____

Section B: There, their and they're

There 50th anniversary party is in August. Their in the middle of all the preparations and arrangments. Some of they're family will be travelling all the way from the USA to join the celebrations so there very excited. Everyone their should have a great time.

Can you spot the words which are used incorrectly in the above sentences?

These words look and sound similar and it can be challenging to decide how to use there, their and they're correctly.

Read the information in each of the examples, test yourself, then go back to the sentences and you should be able to correct them easily.

'There'

This indicates a place, so when you use this word you might be talking about a location or giving directions.

EXAMPLE

There are the dessert moulds I couldn't find.

The chef is over there.

Their

If something is owned by someone, e.g. a chef's knife, you would either use the name of the person to describe this, e.g. 'That's Peter's knife' or alternatively you could say 'That's his knife' referring to Peter, in this example. However, the word 'their' indicates that more than one person possesses ownership of the item.

Tip

Note that ownership of something doesn't have to refer to physical objects.

'They're '

As this word has an apostrophe in it, it indicates that something has been left out. In this case it is the letter 'a'.

This word means 'they (a)re'.

Short-answer questions

Try to put the correct 'there', 'their' or 'they're' in the following sentences.

1. Sometimes _____ is nothing you can do to prevent complaints.

2. Is it possible to get _____ on foot.

3. Health and safety legislation dictates that_____ should be a fire exit clearly visible.

4. _____ going to _____ brother's birthday party next week.

5. Freya said _____ having a great time on holiday.

6. I have _____ rotas for next week.

7. _____ plane is due to land at 08:00.

8. _____ are 5000 people expected to attend _____ concert.

9. They always eat at _____ favorite restaurant on Saturdays.

10. _____ always late, no matter what time we arrange to meet.

Section C: To, two and too

My girlfriend and I are planning a trip two Florence too celebrate her birthday. We are trying two book to tickets with one of the budget airlines. However, this is proving too be difficult as the flights are full. I think we will have two look at other destinations.

Can you spot the incorrect use of words in these sentences?

These words look similar and sound the same so it can be challenging to know how to use to, two and too correctly.

Read the information for each of the examples, test yourself, then go back to the sentences above to see if you are able to correct them.

'To'

To, in this sense, is referred to as a 'preposition' and is a word that provides direction or an indication. A preposition is a word which is used to link words and create phrases, usually referring to a time or place. See the examples of prepositions opposite.

'Two'

Two is the written form of the number '2'.

'Too'

The word 'too' is used to mean the following in sentences:

'in addition'

'also'

'as well'

'very'

'furthermore'

'extremely'.

It is often used to show an excessive extent; beyond what is desirable, fitting or right, e.g., '…too sick to travel', '…too near the fire', 'I am too upset to discuss this at the moment'.

Short-answer questions

Place the correct 'to', 'too' or 'two' in the following sentences.

1. She prefers _____ drink dry white wines rather than sweeter ones.

2. The customers arrived _____ late; lunch service had finished.

3. There are _____ minutes_____ go before the end of the competition.

4. I cannot get _____ the fridge, there are _____ many boxes in the way.

5. _____ of us applied for the job; let's see who they offer it_____.

6. There are _____ many mistakes being made this evening. I want some ideas as _____ how we can stop them from happening.

7. The groom thinks that inviting over 50 guests will be_____ many. He is concerned that it will be _____much, considering his budget.

8. The bride wants the wedding _____be an intimate occasion.

Section D: Where, were and we're

Where thinking about booking a table at the new restaurant in town on Friday evening. We we're going to ask John and Michelle if they would like to join us but I think they're on holiday. We where hoping you could make it though. If you can, were do you suggest we could meet? Where planning to have a drink at the wine bar before we eat if you fancy it but we could meet where is most convenient for you as we know its further for you to come.

Can you spot the incorrect use of words in these sentences?

These words look similar and sound the same so it can be challenging to know how to use where, were and we're correctly.

Read the information for each of the examples, test yourself, then go back to the sentences above to see if you are able to correct them.

Where

This indicates a place or location.

Were

This word presents a sign of something that has happened in the past.

We're

This word means we (a)re.

As this word has an apostrophe in it, it provides a sign that a letter, or letters, has been left out. In this example, it is the letter 'a'.

Short-answer questions

Place the correct 'where, were or we're' in the following sentences.

1. _____ can I find a piping bag to decorate this sponge?

2. _____ you on duty last night?

3. You know London well, _____ would you recommend I should go to eat?

4. It's packed in the restaurant; I think _____ in for a busy evening.

5. I think the waiter has forgotten _____ he's going.

6. _____ you able to see the demonstration from _____ you were sitting?

7. _____ planning a trip to the Maldives for our honeymoon.

8. Could you tell me _____ the manager's office is please?

9. _____ going to have to practice every day if _____ going to win this competition

10. They_____under a great deal of pressure to serve on time.

Now go back to the sentences to see if you can spot the errors.

Unit 5: Punctuation

Apostrophe (') An apostrophe is used to show contraction of two words into one. An apostrophe is placed where the letters have been dropped. (e.g. 'I do not want to be late for work' becomes 'I don't want to be late for work'.)

A possessive apostrophe is used to show possession or relationship.

(e.g. Susan's knives, the children's menu.)

Colon (:) A colon is used to introduce a list, whereas a semicolon is used to introduce a second clause which expands or illustrates the first. (e.g. My food order today is:

2 oranges

1 kiwi

2 pears.

The bread was burnt; the temperature was too high.)

Comma (,) A comma is used to mark a pause in a sentence, or used to separate items in a list. (e.g. The customer ordered two sandwiches, three oranges and four glasses of lemonade.)

Dash (–) A dash may be used to replace brackets; to indicate an afterthought, or to replace other punctuation in informal writing. (e.g. A note to a colleague in the kitchen.)

Ellipsis (...) This signifies a place where something has been omitted or there is a pause or interruption. It is used for economy or style. (e.g. He heard a strange noise in the corridor ... what could it be?)

Exclamation mark (!) A punctuation mark is used at the end of a sentence to show great emotion such as surprise, anger or fear, or to emphasize that something is important. (e.g. Don't drink from this tap!)

Full stop (.) A full stop is the usual end of sentence punctuation.

Exercise 1
Add the correct punctuation to the following menu.

Hotel Buckingham

A La Carte Menu

Welcome to Hotel Buckinghams award winning restaurant where all of the dishes are cooked using the freshest locally sourced ingredients the restaurant is open Monday to Saturday for lunch dinner and afternoon tea We are currently running a lunch special with two courses for £22.95 and three for £25.95

Starters
Smoked Haddock Ravioli

Roast chicken terrine fresh watercress and pickled mushrooms

Chef John Jones famous twice baked cheese souffle

Main Courses

Pan Fried Organic Salmon with Potato Dumplings Braised Lettuce and Pea purée

Roast fillet of beef with potato fondant spinach celeriac purée

Choose from a choice of sauces red wine jus, mustard crème or peppercorn

Chicken in a white wine sauce with spring greens and garlic and chive mash pototo

Ask your waiter for the desert menu and our selection of teas and freshly ground coffees

A 10% gratuity will be added to your bill for tables of six people or more

Unit 6: Writing Formal Letters

It is often a requirement in the hospitality business that formal letters are sent. This may be to customers, suppliers or a person applying for a role within the company.

A formal letter is a method of communication that reflects how you or a business communicates in a formal manner. There are a number of functions and purposes and a letter of this nature should be clear, concise and courteous as well as following a structure. This can be seen below.

Key to Parts of a Formal Letter

a) The sender's address or, if sent by an organization, the letter heading of the company including a company logo.

b) Name, title and company name and address of the person and, if to a company, the company receiving the letter.

c) Date expressed as day, month and year.

d) Heading: indicating what the letter is about.

e) Salutation: Dear Mr/Mrs etc., as the letter is addressed in the name and address line.

f) Introductory paragraph.

g) Middle paragraphs providing details.

h) Closing paragraphs providing an action statement and a courteous close.

i) Complimentary close: Yours sincerely because the recipient's name is used in the salutation. The writer's name and title, leaving space for the writer's signature!

45 The Greenway **(a)**
Kingston-Upon-Thames
KT54 8WE

Ms Jane Smith **(b)**
Restaurant Manager
The Sphere
Camden High Road
London
NW14 2EZ

14 April 2012 **(c)**

Re: Poor Coffee and Service **(d)**

Dear Ms Smith **(e)**

I recently purchased two filter coffees from your restaurant, priced at £3.50 each.

Unfortunately, when my friend and I took our first sips, the coffee was lukewarm at best. **(f)**

I informed the duty manager, Derek Johnson, who informed me that the element in the coffee machine was faulty and there was nothing more he could do. I was most upset by this attitude and asked to speak to the manager but was told that the manager was on leave for the rest of the week. Despite this, I would have expected at least the offer of another drink or a refund. **(g)**

I have returned to your restaurant on several occasions when passing, requesting to speak to the manager but have never managed to do so. However, on my last visit, I was passed your details and informed that I could write to you to express my concerns. For your information, I had previously requested a refund but this was declined on the basis that we had drunk nearly half of the coffee before we raised our complaint. **(g)**

The Supply of Goods and Services Act 1982, states that any service provided in the UK, should be carried out with reasonable care and skill, within a reasonable time, which I agree happened in this case, and at a reasonable cost. As two of these criteria were not met, I would like to request a full reimbursement of the amount paid. **(g)**

I would appreciate a reply within 2 weeks in the hope that this matter can be resolved quickly. **(h)**

L.A. Jenkins **(i)**

Yours sincerely

Mrs Lilly-Anne Jenkins

Answer the following questions.

1. What was the cause of the fault?

    _____

2. What did the purchaser wish would take place next?

    _____

3. Who did she initially complain to?

    _____

4. In what condition should a service be provided?

    _____

5. What is the purpose of the letter?

    _____

6. What is the style/type of this document?

    _____

    _____

7. How much is Mrs Jenkins expecting for a refund?

    _____

8. When should she have a response by?

    _____

Task

Place yourself in the position of the manager of The Sphere Restaurant and, following the guidelines provided above, write a response to Mrs Jenkins.

It is important to show your workings out to indicate how you calculated your answer. Use this workbook to practice the questions and record your answers. Use extra paper if necessary to record your workings out.

Unit 7: General Mathematics

Short-answer questions

Specific instructions to students

- This unit will help you to improve your general mathematical skills.
- Read the following questions and answer all of them in the spaces provided.
- You may not use a calculator.
- You need to show all working.

QUESTION 1

What unit of measurement would you use to measure:

a the amount of cooking oil used in a recipe?

Answer:

_____

b the temperature of an oven (in both metric and imperial units)?

Answer:

_____

c the amount of oil in a deep fryer?

Answer:

_____

d the weight of a freezer?

Answer:

_____

e the speed of a delivery van?

Answer:

_____

f the height of a walk-in fridge?

Answer:

_____

g the cost of a main course dish?

Answer:

_____

QUESTION 2

Give examples of how the following might be used in the hospitality or catering industry:

a percentages

Answer:

_____

b decimals

Answer:

---

c fractions

Answer:

---

d mixed numbers

Answer:

---

e ratios

Answer:

---

f angles

Answer:

QUESTION 3
Convert the following units:

a 12 kilograms to grams

Answer:

---

b 4 tonnes to kilograms

Answer:

---

c 120 centimetres to metres

Answer:

---

d 1140 millilitres to litres

Answer:

---

e 1650 grams to kilograms

Answer:

---

f 18 kilograms to tonnes

Answer:

---

g 13 metres to centimetres

Answer:

---

h 4.5 litres to millilitres

Answer:

QUESTION 4
Write the following in descending order:

0.4   0.04   4.1   40.0   400.00   4.0

Answer:

QUESTION 5
Write the decimal number that is between the following:

a 0.2 and 0.4

Answer:

---

b 1.8 and 1.9

Answer:

---

c 12.2 and 12.8

Answer:

---

d 28.3 and 28.4

Answer:

---

e 101.5 and 103

Answer:

QUESTION 6

Round off the following numbers to two (2) decimal places:

a 12.346

Answer:

b 2.251

Answer:

c 123.897

Answer:

d 688.882

Answer:

e 1209.741

Answer:

QUESTION 7

Estimate the following by approximation:

a 1288 × 19 =

Answer:

b 201 × 20 =

Answer:

c 497 × 12.2 =

Answer:

d 1008 × 10.3 =

Answer:

e 399 × 22 =

Answer:

f 201 − 19 =

Answer:

g 502 − 61 =

Answer:

h 1003 − 49 =

Answer:

i 10 001 − 199 =

Answer:

j 99.99 − 39.8 =

Answer:

QUESTION 8

What do the following add up to?

a £4, £4.99 and £144.95

Answer:

b 8.75, 6.9 and 12.55

Answer:

c 65 mL, 18 mL and 209 mL

Answer:

d 21.3 g, 119 g and 884.65 g

Answer:

QUESTION 9

Subtract the following:

a 2338 from 7117

Answer:

b 1786 from 3112

Answer:

c 5979 from 8014

Answer:

d 11 989 from 26 221

Answer:

e 108 767 from 231 111

Answer:

QUESTION 10

7 / 2177

7 into 2 (too big)

7 into 21 = 3 (21) first calculation 3

7 into 7 = 1 (7) second calculation 1 (31)

7 into 7 = 1 (7) last calculation (311)

Answer = 311

Use the process of division to solve:

a 5589 divided by 9

Answer:

b 4484 divided by 4

Answer:

c 63.9 divided by 0.3

Answer:

d 121.63 divided by 1.2

Answer:

e 466.88 divided by 0.8

Answer:

The following information is provided for Question 11.

To solve using BODMAS, in order from left to right solve the Brackets first, then Of, then Division, then Multiplication, then Addition and lastly Subtraction. The following example has been done for your reference.

EXAMPLE:

Solve $(4 \times 7) \times 2 + 6 - 4$.

STEP 1

Solve the Brackets first: $(4 \times 7) = 28$

STEP 2

No Division so next solve Multiplication: $28 \times 2 = 56$

STEP 3

Addition is next: $56 + 6 = 62$

STEP 4

Subtraction is the last process: $62 - 4 = 58$

FINAL ANSWER:

QUESTION 11

Using BODMAS, solve:

a $(6 \times 9) \times 5 + 7 - 2$

Answer:

---

b $(9 \times 8) \times 4 + 6 - 1$

Answer:

---

c $3 \times (5 \times 7) + 11 - 8$

Answer:

---

d $6 + 9 - 5 \times (8 \times 3)$

Answer:

---

e $9 - 7 + 6 \times 3 + (9 \times 6)$

Answer:

---

f $(4 \times 3) - 6 + 9 \times 4 + (6 \times 7)$

Answer:

---

g $(4 \times 9) - (3 \times 7) + 16 - 11 \times 2$

Answer:

---

h $9 - 4 \times 6 + (6 \times 7) + (8 \times 9) - 23$

Answer:

Section A: Addition

Short-answer questions

Specific instructions to students

- This section will help you to improve your addition skills for basic operations.
- Read the questions below and answer all of them in the spaces provided.
- You may not use a calculator.
- You need to show all working.

QUESTION 1

To make a mixture for a sponge, the recipe requires, add 200 g flour, 15 g sugar and 70 g of egg. How much does the mixture weigh in total?

Answer:

QUESTION 2

A chef uses 2.5 kg, 1.8 kg, 3.3 kg and 15.2 kg of flour for four different mixes. How much flour has been used in total?

Answer:

QUESTION 3

During a stocktake, a commis waiter stocks 327 forks, 368 knives and 723 various other pieces of cutlery. How many pieces of cutlery do they have in stock?

Answer:

QUESTION 4

When delivering pizzas a car is driven 352 km, 459 km, 872 km and 198 km over four consecutive weeks. How far has the car been driven in total?

Answer:

QUESTION 5

A food delivery driver uses the following amounts of diesel over a month: 35.5 litres in week 1, 42.9 litres in week 2, 86.9 litres in week 3 and 66.2 litres in week 4.

a How many litres have been used?

Answer:

b If diesel costs £1.35 per litre, how much would fuel have cost for the month?

Answer:

QUESTION 6

A chef buys a frying pan for £82.50, four paring knives for £116.80 and a mixing bowl for £6.75. How much has been spent?

Answer:

QUESTION 7

A commis chef uses a 20 kg bag of flour to complete three recipes. A total of 2.6 kg is used on one recipe, 5.2 kg is used on another and 4.8 kg is used on the last recipe.

a How much flour has been used?

Answer:

b How much flour is left?

Answer:

QUESTION 8

A chef buys a steamer for £225.80, a chopping board for £26.99 and a new knife set for £88.50. How much has been spent in total?

Answer:

QUESTION 9

Over a period of 3 weeks, a commis chef travels 36 miles, 33 miles, 37 miles and 44 miles to get to and from work. How far has he travelled?

Answer:

QUESTION 10

178 g, 188 g and 93 g of spices are needed to complete some large specialist dishes. How much of the spices are needed in total?

Answer:

Section B: Subtraction

Short-answer questions

Specific instructions to students

- This section will help you to improve your subtraction skills for basic operations.
- Read the following questions and answer all of them in the spaces provided.
- You may not use a calculator.
- You need to show all working.

QUESTION 1

A deep fryer is filled up with cooking oil to its limit of 20 litres. During lunch service 2.2 litres is used, A further 1.7 litres is used during dinner service and 1.1 litres during breakfast service the following morning.

a How much oil is used?

Answer:

b How much oil is left in the vessel?

Answer:

QUESTION 2

If a chef uses 362 g of flour, and another chef uses 169 g, how much more has the first chef used than the second?

Answer:

QUESTION 3

Apprentice chef A uses 24.8 litres of cooking oil in one month, and apprentice chef B uses 14.7 litres in the same month. How much more does chef A use than chef B?

Answer:

QUESTION 4

A chef uses 39 shallots from a box that has 163 shallots. How many are left?

Answer:

QUESTION 5

A bill for a meal comes to £224.65. The manager takes off a discount of £26.48. How much does the bill now come to?

Answer:

QUESTION 6

Over the course of a year, an apprentice chef drives 12 316 km. Of this, 2787 km is for her personal use. What distance was used for work?

Answer:

QUESTION 7

A kitchen uses the following amounts of wine in cooking over 3 months:

Month A – 5.5 litres

Month B – 3.8 litres

Month C – 6.9 litres

a How much wine is used?

Answer:

b How much oil is left from a drum that contained 20 litres of oil to begin with?

Answer:

QUESTION 8

During 1 month, 74 plates were broken. If there was a total of 140 plates at the beginning of the month, how many are now left?

Answer:

QUESTION 9

The odometer of a regional catering manager has a reading of 78 769 before it is then driven for 3 months. Afterwards, it reads 84 231. How many kilometres have been travelled?

Answer:

QUESTION 10

A commis chef uses the following amounts of sauces on three separate jobs: 87 mL, 69 mL and 153 mL. If there were 500 mL of sauce to begin with, how much is left?

Answer:

Section C: Multiplication

Short-answer questions

Specific instructions to students

- This section will help you to improve your multiplication skills for basic operations.
- Read the following questions and answer all of them in the spaces provided.
- You may not use a calculator.
- You need to show all working.

QUESTION 1

A pastry chef can line 30 flan cases per hour, how many flan cases will he line in 3.5 hours?

Answer:

QUESTION 2

If a delivery van travels at 80 km/h, how far will it travel in 8 hours?

Answer:

QUESTION 3

An agency chef uses 8 litres of fuel to get to and from work each day. How much fuel is used if the same trip needs to be completed 26 times?

Answer:

QUESTION 4

When making pizzas a commis chef uses 125 g of onions, 145 g of olives and 180 g of Mozzarella cheese for one pizza. How much of each ingredient would be needed for 14 of the same pizzas?

Answer:

QUESTION 5

1.5 kg of green pepper, 2 kg of red onion and 8 kg of cos lettuce are used for salads in one night at a bistro. How much of each ingredient is needed, if the same salad is made up each night for 14 nights?

Answer:

QUESTION 6

160 bread rolls are used during dinner service in a restaurant. How many bread rolls would you need for 28 nights if the same amount of rolls were needed for each night?

Answer:

QUESTION 7

A mobile chef uses 9 litres of petrol for every 100 km. How much petrol would be used for 400 km?

Answer:

QUESTION 8

On average, a restaurant uses 285 chicken breasts per month. How many would be used over a year? (Note there are 12 months in 1 year.)

Answer:

QUESTION 9

If an apprentice chef uses 3 kg of flour each day for different preparations, how much flour is used over 28 days (4 weeks)?

Answer:

QUESTION 10

If a chef prepares 110 canapés per hour for 5 hours, how many canapés will she produce?

Answer:

Section D: Division

Short-answer questions

Specific instructions to students

- This section will help you to improve your division skills for basic operations.
- Read the following questions and answer all of them in the spaces provided.
- You may not use a calculator.
- You need to show all working.

QUESTION 1

A chef has a 25 kg bag of strong flour to make fresh bread.

a How many batches of bread can be produced if each standard batch requires 3 kg of flour?

Answer:

b How much flour is left over?

Answer:

QUESTION 2

A sous chef earns £785 for working a 5-day week. How much does he earn per day?

Answer:

QUESTION 3

A chef produces 140 litres of chicken stock and stores it in 2-litre containers. How many containers will he use in total?

Answer:

QUESTION 4

A delivery lorry covers 780 miles in a 5-day week. On average, how many miles are travelled each day?

Answer:

QUESTION 5

The total weight of 4 sacks of sugar is 88 kilograms. How much does each sack weigh?

Answer:

QUESTION 6

A grocery delivery vehicle covers 925 miles over a 7-day period. How much distance is covered, on average, each day?

Answer:

QUESTION 7

During a yearly stocktake, an apprentice chef counts 648 packets of spice mix. Each box contains 12 packets.

a How many boxes are there?

Answer:

b Are any boxes left over?

Answer:

QUESTION 8

480 new steak knives are ordered for a restaurant. If there are 6 in each box, how many boxes are there?

Answer:

QUESTION 9

A delivery lorry carries 644 cans of soup to various contracts. The cans are stored in 6 cabinets.

a How many cans are in each cabinet?

Answer:

b Are there any cans left over?

Answer:

QUESTION 10

4 kg of cake mixture is needed to make 244 cupcakes. How much mixture is needed for each cupcake?

Answer:

Section A: Addition

Short-answer questions

Specific instructions to students

- This section will help you to improve your addition skills when working with decimals.
- Read the following questions and answer all of them in the spaces provided.
- You may not use a calculator.
- You need to show all working.

QUESTION 1

A set of four knives costs £56.50 and a chopping board costs £22.75.

a If you buy the knives and the chopping board, how much will you pay in total?

Answer:

_____

b How much change will have left over from £100.00?

Answer:

_____

QUESTION 2

A head chef purchases the following: a uniform for £89.95, safety shoes for £39.95 and several neckties for £24.55.

a How much has she spent?

Answer:

_____

b How much change does she receive from £200.00?

Answer:

_____

QUESTION 3

A measuring cup holds 52 g of sugar. Another holds 52.33 g. What is the total sugar weight?

Answer:

_____

QUESTION 4

A cook's baking tray is 60.25 cm long and another is 82.48 cm. What is the total length of both?

Answer:

_____

QUESTION 5

A chef buys the following to make spaghetti carbonara for a large party of guests:

5 kilograms of spaghetti for £8.99

2 litres of cream for £6.50

1 litre of extra virgin olive oil for £7.25

2 kilograms of pancetta for £31.50

30 eggs for £5.05

750 grams of Parmesan cheese for £14.40

a What is the total cost?

Answer:

_____

b If the chef uses a £100 note to pay for it all, how much will he have left?

Answer:

_____

QUESTION 6

If a delivery lorry travels 65.8 km, 36.5 km, 22.7 km and 89.9 km over 4 days, how far has it travelled in total?

Answer:

_____

QUESTION 7

What is the total length of a frying pan with a handle length of 5.5 cm and a plate 27.8 cm long?

Answer:

_____

QUESTION 8

A cup has a diameter of 52.4 mm and another has a diameter of 50.8 mm. What is the total diameter length of both cups?

Answer:

QUESTION 9

A chef completes three orders. The totals are as follows for each order: £45.80 for the first order, £130.65 for the second and £6.45 for the last order.

a How much is the total bill?

Answer:

b How much change will be needed if £200 is received for all three orders?

Answer:

QUESTION 10

A customer orders the following for dinner:

soup (£4.90)

a main course of whiting (£28.50)

chocolate dessert (£5.50)

a What does the total bill come to?

Answer:

b How much change will be given if the customer pays with a £50 note?

Answer:

Section B: Subtraction

Short-answer questions

Specific instructions to students

- This section will help you to improve your subtraction skills when working with decimals.
- Read the following questions and answer all of them in the spaces provided.
- You may not use a calculator.
- You need to show all working.

QUESTION 1

A kitchen assistant preparing the ingredients to make some créme caramels pours 250 mL from a 2 L bottle of milk. How much milk is left?

Answer:

QUESTION 2

If a chef cuts off 2.5 cm of fat from the end of a steak that is 31.4 cm long, how much steak is left?

Answer:

QUESTION 3

A chef completes an order that costs £82.20. The restaurant then gives a discount of £8.20 as the patron has a discount voucher.

a How much is the final cost?

Answer:

b The patron pays £100.00 for the order. How much change will the restaurant need to give the patron?

Answer:

QUESTION 4

An apprentice chef works 38 hours and earns £245.60. £28.85 is deducted for tax. How much pay does the chef take home?

Answer:

QUESTION 5

A new 750 mL bottle of cooking oil is used over two nights in a bistro. The total amount of oil used is 88.5 mL. How much oil is left in the bottle?

Answer:

QUESTION 6

A frying pan has a diameter of 39.5 cm, and another pan has a diameter of 28.5 cm. What is the difference in length between the two?

Answer:

QUESTION 7

A saucepan has a depth of 25.5 cm. It is filled to a height of 17.5 cm with soup. What height is left in the pan?

Answer:

QUESTION 8

A chef has a 4 L can of sesame oil. The following amounts are used over three different lunch sittings:

Day 1: 1285 mL

Day 2: 1160 mL

Day 3: 1300 mL

a How much oil is used in total?

Answer:

b How much is left?

Answer:

QUESTION 9

A bill includes £35.50 for two meals, £7.50 for a dessert and £14.45 for three coffees. If the bill is paid with two £50 notes, how much change is given?

Answer:

QUESTION 10

A set of knives is purchased at a cost of £80.50. If it is paid for with four £20 notes and one £10 note, how much change is given?

Answer:

Section C: Multiplication

Short-answer questions

Specific instructions to students

- This section will help you to improve your multiplication skills when working with decimals.
- Read the following questions and answer all of them in the spaces provided.
- You may not use a calculator.
- You need to show all working.

QUESTION 1

A saucepan costs £29.95.

a How much will a set of six of the same pans cost?

Answer:

b What is the change from £200.00?

Answer:

QUESTION 2

An apprentice chef works 16 hours over a weekend. If he gets paid £6.50, how much will he get in total?

Answer:

QUESTION 3

A stores assistant replaces six spice containers that cost £6.50 each, and then purchases four bottles of sweet chilli at £3.95 per bottle.

a What is the total cost?

Answer:

b What change is needed from £60.00?

Answer:

QUESTION 4

A party of six dine at a restaurant that charges £22.50 per person for their fixed priced menu.

a How much is the total food bill?

Answer:

b The diners tip £15.00. How much change will they receive from £150.00?

Answer:

QUESTION 5

Nine cocktails are ordered priced at £4.50 each.

a How much is the total cost?

Answer:

b How much change is received from £50.00?

Answer:

QUESTION 6

A customer orders three steamed dim sims. Each dim sim costs £2.20.

a How much does it cost in total?

Answer:

b How much change will be need from £10.00?

Answer:

QUESTION 7

A canteen buys 120 paninis for £1.85 each. What is the total cost?

Answer:

QUESTION 8

A hotel orders 50 dozen oysters at £5.50 per dozen. What is the total bill?

Answer:

QUESTION 9

3400 dinner rolls are purchased for a major function. If each one costs 15 pence, what is the total bill?

Answer:

QUESTION 10

A sous chef earns £180.65 per day. How much does he earn in 5 days?

Answer:

Section D: Division

Short-answer questions

Specific instructions to students

- This section will help you to improve your division skills when working with decimals.
- Read the following questions and answer all of them in the spaces provided.
- You may not use a calculator.
- You need to show all working.

QUESTION 1

6.6 litres of vegetable oil is used over 6 days. How much is used each day?

Answer:

QUESTION 2

A chef earns £990.50 for 5 days work. How much is earned per day?

Answer:

QUESTION 3

A dinner bill totals £332.70 for 8 people. How much will it cost each person if they split the bill evenly?

Answer:

QUESTION 4

A bill totals £440.85 for 12 people. How much is it per person?

Answer:

QUESTION 5

A kitchen makes 570 meals over 3 days. How many meals are produced, on average, per day?

Answer:

QUESTION 6

A private caterer drives 889.95 km in 12 days to cater for different clients. How far is travelled, on average, each day?

Answer:

QUESTION 7

A sous chef uses 11 L of milk to make 257 portions of chocolate bavarois. How much milk is used for each dessert?

Answer:

QUESTION 8

To make 14 portions of ciabatta dough, 2 kg of flour is needed. How many grams of flour is used in four portions?

Answer:

QUESTION 9

It costs £93.95 to fill the 52-litre fuel tank of a delivery van. How much does the fuel cost per litre?

Answer:

QUESTION 10

A 50 m roll of cling film costs £23.60. How much does it cost per metre?

Answer:

Section A: Addition

Short-answer questions

Specific instructions to students

- This section is designed to help you to improve your addition skills when working with fractions.
- Read the following questions and answer all of them in the spaces provided.
- You may not use a calculator.
- You need to show all working.

QUESTION 1

$\frac{1}{4} + \frac{2}{4} = ?$

Answer:

QUESTION 2

$1\frac{1}{3} + 1\frac{1}{3} = ?$

Answer:

QUESTION 3

A chef pours $\frac{1}{3}$ of a bottle of olive oil into a container. Another $\frac{1}{4}$ is added from another bottle. How much in total is there? Provide your answer as a fraction.

Answer:

QUESTION 4

One jug of coffee is $\frac{1}{3}$ full. Another is $\frac{1}{2}$ full. How much coffee is there in total? Express your answer as a fraction of a full can.

Answer:

QUESTION 5

An apprentice has $1\frac{2}{3}$ cans of beer when making a carbonade of beef. She tops this up with $1\frac{1}{2}$ more cans of beer. How much beer is there in total? Write your answer as a fraction.

Answer:

Section B: Subtraction

Short-answer questions

Specific instructions to students

- This section is designed to help you to improve your subtraction skills when working with fractions.
- Read the following questions and answer all of them in the spaces provided.
- You may not use a calculator.
- You need to show all working.

QUESTION 1

Solve $\frac{2}{3} - \frac{1}{4}$

Answer:

QUESTION 2

$2\frac{2}{3} - 1\frac{1}{4} =$

Answer:

QUESTION 3

A chef prepares a cake mix. If there is $\frac{1}{2}$ a carton of milk and a $\frac{1}{4}$ of the carton is used during the preparation, how much milk is left in the carton (express your answer as a fraction of the carton)?

Answer:

QUESTION 4

A commis chef has $2\frac{1}{2}$ bottles of red wine. If $1\frac{1}{3}$ is used in two separate dishes, how much wine is left?

Answer:

QUESTION 5

An apprentice chef has $2\frac{3}{4}$ small bottles of red pepper essence, $1\frac{1}{2}$ is used during lunch service. How much is left in total as a fraction?

Answer:

Section C: Multiplication

Short-answer questions

Specific instructions to students

- This section is designed to help you to improve your multiplication skills when working with fractions.
- Read the following questions and answer all of them in the spaces provided.
- You may not use a calculator.
- You need to show all working.

QUESTION 1

Solve $\frac{2}{4} \times \frac{2}{3}$

Answer:

QUESTION 2

$2\frac{2}{3} \times 1\frac{1}{2} =$

Answer:

QUESTION 3

A sous chef trims the fat from two steaks, A strip of $8\frac{1}{2}$ cm of fat is taken off each. What is the total length of fat in cm that was taken off the steak?

Answer:

QUESTION 4

A kitchen has 4 spice jars that are all $\frac{3}{4}$ full of oregano.

How much oregano is there in total? Express your answer in bottles.

Answer:

QUESTION 5

A function room is $\frac{2}{3}$ full on four separate evenings. Over the four nights, how full is the room in total? Express your answer as a fraction of the maximum capacity.

Answer:

Section D: Division

Short-answer questions

Specific instructions to students

- This section is designed to help you to improve your division skills when working with fractions.
- Read the following questions and answer all of them in the spaces provided.
- You may not use a calculator.
- You need to show all working.

QUESTION 1

Solve: $\frac{2}{3} \div \frac{1}{4}$

Answer:

QUESTION 2

Solve: $2\frac{3}{4} \div 1\frac{1}{3}$

Answer:

QUESTION 3

An apprentice chef has four containers of flour in the kitchen. If they need to be divided into three larger containers, how much of the each container will go into the new containers?

Answer:

QUESTION 4

A commis chef has $1\frac{2}{3}$ cans of tomatoes. If they are to be used in three dishes, how much will be used in each dish?

Answer:

QUESTION 5

A chef uses $2\frac{2}{3}$ bottles of peanut oil over 2 days. How much as a fraction is used on each day?

Answer:

Unit 11: Percentages

Short-answer questions

Specific instructions to students

- In this unit, you will be able to practice and improve your skills in working out percentages. Percentages are used regularly in the hospitality industry to judge financial performance and analyze trends.
- Read the following questions and answer all of them in the spaces provided.
- You should not use a calculator.
- You need to show all working.

> **10% rule: Move the decimal one place to the left to get 10%.**

EXAMPLE

10% of £45.00 would be £4.50

QUESTION 1

Due to the slow speed of service, a restaurant manager offers diners a discount of 10% from their bill of £220.00.

a How much is 10% of the bill?

Answer:

_____

b If this is deducted from the bill, how much is the reduced bill?

Answer:

_____

QUESTION 2

The cost of five new saucepans is £249.00. A chef negotiates 10% off the cost price. What price did the chef pay?

Answer:

_____

QUESTION 3

A hotel manager buys a replacement air conditioner for £1198.50.

a If he was given a 10% discount, how much is the discount?

Answer:

_____

b How much does the air conditioner cost after subtracting the discount?

Answer:

_____

QUESTION 4

A chef buys punnets of raspberries for £8.80. She gets a 5% discount. How much does she pay? (Hint: find 10%, halve it and then subtract it from £8.80.)

Answer:

_____

QUESTION 5

A food stores technician buys three storage bins for £20, a set of weighing scales for £69 and a vacuum packing machine for £169.

a How much is paid in total?

Answer:

_____

b How much is paid after a 10% discount?

Answer:

_____

QUESTION 6

The following items are purchased for a staff restaurant: a carving knife for £39.99, a knife sharpener for £19.99, five chopping boards for £19.99, a digital thermometer for £12.99, a non-stick frying pan for £49.99 and 25 m of cling film for £4.99.

a What is the total cost?

Answer:

_____

b What is the final cost after a 5% discount?

Answer:

_____

QUESTION 7

A supplier offers 20% off the price of a range of crockery.

a If two plates cost £59.80 before the discount, how much will they cost after the discount is applied?

Answer:

_____

b What is the total discount?

Answer:

_____

QUESTION 8

An equipment supplier discounts ladles by 15%. If the regular retail price is £15.50 each, what is the discounted price?

Answer:

_____

QUESTION 9

A dry goods supplier sells 1kg of ground almonds at £6.90 at trade. The supplier offers 20% for regular customers. How much will it cost at the discounted price?

Answer:

_____

QUESTION 10

A soup blender, usually sold at £120.00, is promoted at a discounted price of 30%. How much will it cost at the discounted price?

Answer:

_____

Question 11

A chef prepares to make a Moroccan spiced pie using the following recipe. She needs to increase the quantities of the ingredients to make a Moroccan spiced pie that is 50% larger than the original recipe. Calculate the quantities of the ingredients she will need.

Recipe

- 2 tsp each coriander and cumin seeds **(Spice)**
- 1 tsp **paprika**, plus extra for dusting **(Spice)**
- ½ tsp ground **cinnamon (Spice)**
- 150ml/¼ pint **olive oil (Liquid)**
- 140g shelled pistachios **(Fruit/nut)**
- 1 pound pack dried **cranberries (Fruit/Nut)**
- 400g can chickpeas, drained and rinsed **(Vegetable/herb)**
- 5 ounces **garlic cloves (Vegetable/herb)**
- 1 tsp ground **cumin (Spice)**
- 3 tbsp lemon juice **(Liquid)**
- 4lb 3oz chopped fresh coriander **(Vegetable/herb)**
- 3lb 2oz butter **(Dairy)**
- 24 large sheets of filo pastry **(Pastry)**
- 2 oz lemon wedges to serve **(Fruit/Nut)**

Total each category, converting all ingredients into metric weights and measures (grams/kilograms, ml/litres) and calculate the percentage each category makes of the total recipe.

Use the following conversions in your calculations:

- 25g = 1oz
- 1 pound = 16oz
- 1tsp = 5g
- 1tbsp = 15ml
- 1 sheet filo pastry = 15g

Spice_____

_____

Dairy_____

_____

Liquid_____

_____

Fruit/Nut_____

_____

Vegetable/Herb_____

_____

Pastry_____

Unit 12: Measurement Conversions

Section A: General measurement conversions

QUESTION 1

How many millilitres are there in 1 litre?

Answer:

_____

QUESTION 2

How many millilitres are there in 3 litres?

Answer:

_____

QUESTION 3

How many millilitres are there in 11 litres?

Answer:

_____

QUESTION 4

A measuring cup has 40 mL of cream poured into it. A further 65 mL is added, and then finally 55 mL more is added. How much in cream is there in total?

Answer:

_____

QUESTION 5

A recipe requires 500 mL of stock, 25 mL of soy sauce and 250 mL of water. How many millilitres of liquid is this in total?

Answer:

_____

QUESTION 6

A saucepan contains 3500 mL of fish stock. How much sauce is there in litres?

Answer:

_____

QUESTION 7

A sugar container holds 1500 g of sugar. Express this in kilograms

Answer:

_____

QUESTION 8

A sack of rice weighs 10 000 grams. How much does it weigh in kilograms?

Answer:

_____

QUESTION 9

A container of carrot and coriander soup cans weighs 8 kg. How much does it weigh in grams?

Answer:

_____

QUESTION 10

A restaurant manager needs to order new tablecloths for tables in the restaurant. Each table measures 180 cm in length and 120 cm across the side. The manager needs to calculate how far it is around the perimeter of the table?

Answer:

_____

Section B: Converting recipe measurements

Use the measurement table below to convert the ingredients to their metric or imperial equivalents in the Beef Wellington and Sweet and Sour Pork recipes.

Conversions table

1 gram (g) = 1000 milligrams (mg)	1 kilogram (kg) = 1000 grams (g)
1 pound (lb) = 16 ounces (oz)	1 gram (g)= 0.035 ounces (oz)
1 stone (st) = 14 pounds (lb)	1 teaspoon (tsp) = 5 grams (g)
1 ounce (oz) = 28 grams (g)	1 fluid ounce (fl oz) = 28 millilitres (mL)
1 tablespoon (tbsp) = 3 teaspoons (tsp)	1 egg = 2 ounces (oz)
1 millilitre (mL) = 1.2 grams (g)	1 litre (L)= 1000 millilitres (mL)
240 grams (g) = 1 cup	1 onion = 105 000 mlligrams (mg)
1 tea spoon (tsp) = 5 millilitres (ml) liquid	1 table spoon (tbsp) = 15 millilitres (ml) liquid

Beef Wellington recipe

- 3 tbsp Olive oil

- 1 lb Chestnut mushrooms, include some wild ones if you like

- 2oz Butter

- 1 tbsp Sprig fresh thyme

- 4fl oz Dry white wine

- 2 lb 3 oz slices Prosciutto

- 1lb 2oz pack Puff pastry, thawed if frozen

- 1 tsp Flour, for dusting

- 2 Eggs beaten with 1 tsp water

- a good Beef fillet (preferably Aberdeen Angus) of around 2lb 4oz

Sweet and Sour Pork recipe

- 400g Pork fillet

- 1 tbsp Sake

- 50g Plain flour (sifted)

- 1 Egg (medium), lightly beaten

- 2 Red peppers, quartered and deseeded

- Spring onions (bunch), trimmed

- 225g Bamboo shoots (canned) drained

- 225g Pineapple chunks (canned) in juice

- 1 tbsp Cornflour

- 1 tbsp Soy sauce

- 1 tbsp Sunflower oil for deep frying

Sweet and Sour Sauce

- 2 tbsp Cornflour

- 100ml Water

- 60 ml Soft brown sugar

- 30 ml Soy sauce

- 90ml Rice or white wine vinegar

- 30ml Tomato ketchup

Section A: Circumference

Short-answer questions

Specific instructions to students

- This section is designed to help you to both improve your skills and to increase your speed in measuring the circumference of a round object.
- Read the following questions and answer all of them in the spaces provided.
- You may not use a calculator.
- You need to show all working.

$$C = \pi \times d$$

where:

C = circumference

π = 3.14

d = diameter

EXAMPLE

Find the circumference of a plate with a diameter of 30 cm.

$C = \pi \times d$

Therefore, $C = 3.14 \times 30$

$= 94.2$ cm

QUESTION 1

Find the circumference of a saucepan with a diameter of 20 cm.

Answer:

QUESTION 2

Calculate the circumference of a soup tureen with a diameter of 15 cm.

Answer:

QUESTION 3

Determine the circumference of a frying pan with a diameter of 32 cm.

Answer:

QUESTION 4

Find the circumference of a mixing bowl with a diameter of 18 cm.

Answer:

QUESTION 5

Calculate the circumference of a plastic lid with a diameter of 12 cm.

Answer:

QUESTION 6

Find the circumference of a saucepan with a diameter of 38.8 cm.

Answer:

QUESTION 7

Determine the circumference of a container with a diameter of 15.6 cm.

Answer:

QUESTION 8

Calculate the circumference of a wine barrel with a diameter of 14.3 cm.

Answer:

QUESTION 9

Find the circumference of a cake board with a diameter of 12.9 cm.

Answer:

QUESTION 10

Determine the circumference of a main-course plate with a diameter of 18.8 cm.

Answer:

Section B: Diameter

Short-answer questions

Specific instructions to students

- This section is designed to help you to both improve your skills and to increase your speed in measuring the diameter of a round object.
- Read the following questions and answer all of them in the spaces provided.
- You may not use a calculator.
- You need to show all working.

Diameter (*d*) of a circle = $\frac{circumference}{\pi (3.14)}$

EXAMPLE

Find the diameter of a cooking pot with a circumference of 80 cm.

$d = \frac{800}{3.14}$

$= 254.78$ cm

QUESTION 1

Find the diameter of a service platter with a circumference of 90 cm.

Answer:

QUESTION 2

Determine the diameter of a saucepan with a circumference of 16 cm.

Answer:

QUESTION 3

Find the diameter of a dessert plate with a circumference of 20 cm.

Answer:

QUESTION 4

Calculate the diameter of a stock pot with a circumference of 60 cm.

Answer:

QUESTION 5

Determine the diameter of a circular revolving service counter with a circumference of 430 cm.

Answer:

QUESTION 6

Find the diameter of a frying pan with a circumference of 81.8 cm.

Answer:

QUESTION 7

Calculate the diameter of a glass bowl with a circumference of 22.4 cm.

Answer:

QUESTION 8

Determine the diameter of a round table with a circumference of 280.08 cm.

Answer:

QUESTION 9

Find the diameter of a pasta dish with a circumference of 62.3 cm.

Answer:

QUESTION 10

Determine the diameter of a gateau with a circumference of 68.8 cm.

Answer:

Section C: Area

Short-answer questions

Specific instructions to students

- This section is designed to help you to both improve your skills and to increase your speed in measuring surface area.
- Read the following questions and answer all of them in the spaces provided.
- You may not use a calculator.
- You need to show all working.

> Area = length × breadth and is given in square units.
> = *l* × *b*

QUESTION 1

The dimensions of a kitchen are 30 m by 12.8 m. What is the total area of the kitchen?

Answer:

QUESTION 2

A canteen measures 20 m by 13 m. What is the total area?

Answer:

QUESTION 3

The area of a walk-in refrigerator area is 2.85 m by 1.65 m. What is the total area?

Answer:

QUESTION 4

If a bistro kitchen area is 4.5 m by 1.8 m, what is the total area?

Answer:

QUESTION 5

What is the total area of a dining room that measures 13 m by 9 m?

Answer:

QUESTION 6

A function centre measures 35 m by 30 m. What is the total area?

Answer:

QUESTION 7

The storage area of a delivery lorry is 2.06 m by 2.07 m, what is the total area?

Answer:

QUESTION 8

A cold room is 6.53 m by 3.27 m. What is the floor area?

Answer:

QUESTION 9

A washing up area is 3.2 m by 1.6 m. What is the total area?

Answer:

QUESTION 10

A trailer that transports food is 8.9 m long and 2.6 m wide. How much floor area can it accommodate?

Answer:

Section D: Volume of a cube

Short-answer questions

Specific instructions to students

- This section is designed to help you to both improve your skills and to increase your speed in calculating volumes of rectangular or square objects.
- Read the following questions and answer all of them in the spaces provided.
- You may not use a calculator.
- You need to show all working.

> **Volume = length × width × height and is given in cubic units.**
> $$= l \times w \times h$$

QUESTION 1

How many cubic metres are there in a storage area 13 m long, 5 m wide and 4 m high?

Answer:

QUESTION 2

A grocery delivery vehicle has the dimensions of 8 m length, 3 m width and 4 m height. How many cubic metres are available?

Answer:

QUESTION 3

A cold room is 8 m long by 3 m wide by 2 m high, how many cubic metres are there?

Answer:

QUESTION 4

A steaming tray measures 22 cm × 18 cm × 5 cm. How many cubic centimetres can it hold?

Answer:

QUESTION 5

An apprentice uses a roasting tray with the following dimensions: 600 mm × 150 mm × 100 mm. How many cubic millimetres have been made?

Answer:

QUESTION 6

If a freezer unit in a kitchen measures 1.2 m × 600 m × 500 m, what cubic area in metres is available to use for storing frozen goods?

Answer:

QUESTION 7

A box is 1 m long, 60 cm wide and 75 cm tall. How many cubic centimetres are available for storing cans of fruit?

Answer:

QUESTION 8

The chilled storage area of an ice-cream delivery vehicle is 1.4 m × 1.4 m × 880 cm. What is the cubic area?

Answer:

QUESTION 9

A freezer van has the following dimensions: 2.75 m high, 2.35 m wide and 3.6 m long. What is its total volume in cubic metres?

Answer:

QUESTION 10

A kitchen has a larder that is 3.8 m × 3.8 m × 2.5 m. How many cubic metres are there?

Answer:

Section E: Volume of a cylinder

Short-answer questions

Specific instructions to students

- This section is designed to help you to both improve your skills and to increase your speed in calculating the volumes of cylinder-shaped objects.
- Read the following questions and answer all of them in the spaces provided.
- You may not use a calculator.
- You need to show all working.

> Calculate your answers in both cm³ and m³ to 3 decimal places.
> Volume of a cylinder (V_c) = π (3.14) × r^2
> (radius × radius) × height
> $V_c = \pi \times r^2 \times h$

QUESTION 1

What is the volume of a vegetable-oil drum that has a radius of 45 cm and a height of 140 cm?

Answer:

QUESTION 2

What is the volume of a can of chocolate spray that has a radius of 3 cm and a height of 20 cm?

Answer:

QUESTION 3

A canister used for sugar has a radius of 4 cm and a height of 11 cm. What volume can it hold?

Answer:

QUESTION 4

A coffee container has a radius of 12.5 cm and a height of 28 cm. How much coffee can it hold?

Answer:

QUESTION 5

An oil drum can has a radius of 15 cm and a height of 26 cm. What is its volume?

Answer:

QUESTION 6

A gas bottle used for a BBQ has a radius of 17 cm and a height of 30 cm. How much gas can it hold?

Answer:

QUESTION 7

A container of vegetable oil gets poured into three containers. Each container has a radius of 8 cm and a height of 40 cm.

a What is the volume of each container?

Answer:

b What is the volume of all three containers in total?

Answer:

QUESTION 8

A container used for ice cream has a radius of 10.5 cm and a height of 15 cm.

a What is its volume?

Answer:

b If you use half on one dinner session, how much is left?

Answer:

QUESTION 9

A can of tomato purée has a radius of 11 cm and a height of 22 cm.

a What is its volume?

Answer:

b If you use half, how much is left?

Answer:

QUESTION 10

A chef uses a can of fish oil that has a radius of 6 cm and a height of 18 cm. What is its volume?

Answer:

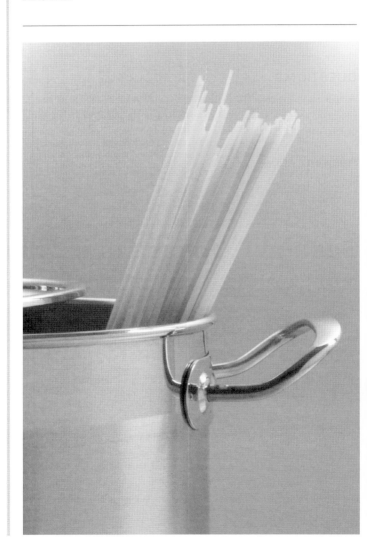

Unit 14: Earning Wages

Short-answer questions
Specific instructions to students

- This unit will help you to calculate how much a job is worth and how long you need to complete the job.
- Read the following questions and answer all of them in the spaces provided.
- You may not use a calculator.
- You need to show all working.

QUESTION 1

An apprentice chef earns £248.50 net per week. How much does she earn per year? (Note there are 52 weeks in a year.)

Answer:

QUESTION 2

A commis chef starts the lunch shift at 10.00 a.m. and stops for a break at 1.30 p.m. He starts again at 2.00 p.m., then finishes the shift at 4.15 p.m. How many hours and minutes has he worked?

Answer:

QUESTION 3

A sommelier earns £15.50 an hour and works a 38-hour week.

a. How much is her gross earnings (that is, before tax)?

b. How much are her net earnings after tax at 30%?

Answer:

QUESTION 4

Over a week, the takings in a restaurant are as follows: £465.80, £2 490.50, £556.20, £1 560.70 and £990.60. What are the total takings?

Answer:

QUESTION 5

A chef in a fast-food restaurant needs the following times to cook five orders: 34 minutes, 18 minutes, 7 minutes, 14 minutes and 9 minutes. How much time has been spent cooking the orders?

Answer:

QUESTION 6

An apprentice needs to prepare food for the evening service. The tasks take $3\frac{1}{2}$ hours to complete. If the rate of pay is £8.60 an hour, how much will be earned during this time?

Answer:

QUESTION 7

A lunch service takes $3\frac{1}{2}$ hours to complete. If the chef is getting paid £24.80 per hour, what is the total amount earned during this time?

Answer:

QUESTION 8

A buffet needs to be prepared in advance for a function. If it takes 3.5 hours to prepare the buffet, 1.5 hours to prepare and decorate the tables and 1/2 hour to prepare drinks, how long has it taken in total?

Answer:

QUESTION 9

A waiter starts work at 7.00 a.m. serving breakfast and works until 3.30 p.m. she had a morning break for 20 minutes, a lunch break for 60 minutes and an afternoon break of 20 minutes.

a How much time has she spent on breaks?

Answer:

b How much time has been spent working?

Answer:

QUESTION 10

The total cost of a function comes to £2850.50. If it took organizers 12 hours to prepare, serve and clean up afterwards, how much is the cost per hour?

Answer:

QUESTION 11

Fill in the gaps on the timesheet, using the instructions and information below.

Luke works a 5-hour shift.

Micheal works for 4.5 hours.

What time does Sarah sign out?

Emma works for 6 hours and 45 minutes and gets paid £2.50 less than Micheal.

Joe earns £1.75 more per hour than Luke and works for 7.5 hours with a 1/2 hour unpaid break in the middle of his shift.

Name	Time in	Time out	Rate of pay	Total
Luke	10:00		£6.50	
Micheal		12:30	£10.45	47.03
Sarah	7:45		£7.50	£33.75
Emma		16:00		
Joe	13:50			

Section A: Introducing square numbers

Short-answer questions

Specific instructions to students

- This section is designed to help you to both improve your skills and to increase your speed in squaring numbers.
- Read the following questions and answer all of them in the spaces provided.
- You may not use a calculator.
- You need to show all working.

> **Any number squared is multiplied by itself.**

EXAMPLE

4 squared $= 4^2 = 4 \times 4 = 16$

QUESTION 1

$6^2 =$

Answer:

QUESTION 2

$8^2 =$

Answer:

QUESTION 3

$12^2 =$

Answer:

QUESTION 4

$3^2 =$

Answer:

QUESTION 5

$7^2 =$

Answer:

QUESTION 6

$11^2 =$

Answer:

QUESTION 7

$10^2 =$

Answer:

QUESTION 8

$9^2 =$

Answer:

QUESTION 9

$2^2 =$

Answer:

QUESTION 10

$4^2 =$

Answer:

QUESTION 11

$5^2 =$

Answer:

Section B: Applying square numbers to the trade

Worded practical problems

Specific instructions to students

- This section is designed to help you to both improve your skills and to increase your speed in calculating volumes of rectangular or square objects. The worded questions make the content relevant to everyday situations.
- Read the following questions and answer all of them in the spaces provided.
- You may not use a calculator.
- You need to show all working.

QUESTION 1

A bistro cook sets aside an area for food preparation. It measures 2.8 m². What area does it take up?

Answer:

QUESTION 2

A dining area measures 5.2 m². What is the total area?

Answer:

QUESTION 3

The dimensions of a function room in a hotel are 12.6 m². What is the total area?

Answer:

QUESTION 4

A maître d' works in a dining area that is 15 m². How much area is in the room?

Answer:

QUESTION 5

A front-of-house manager works at restaurant with a floor area of 23 m² where patrons sit and dine. The bar measures 3 m² . How much area is left for the manager to look after?

Answer:

QUESTION 6

A pastry cook has a sheet of filo pastry that is 120 cm × 120 cm. How much is the total area?

Answer:

QUESTION 7

A baker cuts out choux pastry that measures 50 cm × 50 cm. What is the total area of the pastry?

Answer:

QUESTION 8

A baking tray measures 56 cm × 56 cm. What is the total area of the baking paper required to cover the whole tray?

Answer:

QUESTION 9

A convention centre function room measures 120 m × 120 m. How many square metres does the room take up?

Answer:

QUESTION 10

A café has an outside area that measures 13 m × 13 m. What area does the outside section take up?

Answer:

Unit 16: Ratios

Short-answer questions

Specific instructions to students

- This section is designed to help to improve your skills in calculating and simplifying ratios.
- Read the following questions below and answer all of them in the spaces provided.
- You need to show all working.
- You may not use a calculator.
- Reduce the ratios to the simplest or lowest form.

QUESTION 1

A batch of cake mixture has ingredients with the following ratios: 4 parts dry ingredients to 1 part wet ingredients. If you have 48 parts of dry, how many parts of wet would you need?

Answer:

QUESTION 2

A fruit crumble is made up of 25% crumble mix and 75% mixed fruits. What is the lowest ratio of crumble mix to fruit

Answer:

QUESTION 3

A fruit juice drink needs to be made up for lunch diners at a bistro. A total of 10 litres need to be made up. If the ratio of the mix is 4 parts water to 1 part cordial, how many litres of water and cordial are needed to make up the 10 litres?

Answer:

QUESTION 4

A bottle of salad dressing contains reconstituted vinegar and oil at a ratio of 20% to 80% respectively.

a What is the ratio of the two ingredients?

Answer:

b What would be the lowest ratio of the two?

Answer:

QUESTION 5

A tropical fruit juice mixture contains 40% orange juice, 25% mango juice, 20% pineapple juice and the remainder is water.

a What percentage is made up of water?

Answer:

b What % do the juices make up?

Answer:

QUESTION 6

A soup mix contains 35% stock, 12% packet mix and the rest is water. A vegetable broth is made of 10% carrot, 8% French beans, 6% leeks, 8% turnip, 9% peas, 6% onions with the remainder being stock.

a What percentage is made up of the stock?

Answer:

b What percentage is the water and the stock added together?

Answer:

QUESTION 7

A 2-litre cordial bottle contains 21 g of carbohydrate and 7 mg of sodium. What is the ratio, of carbohydrate to sodium in the cordial? (remember 1 g = 1000 mg)

Answer:

QUESTION 8

A 2-litre cordial bottle and a 2-litre orange juice bottle both list the number of servings per package as part of their nutritional information. If there are 40 servings per cordial bottle and 10 servings per orange juice bottle, what is the comparative ratio of the two?

Answer:

QUESTION 9

A 2-litre cordial bottle, a 2-litre orange juice bottle and a 2-litre soft drink bottle have the following servings per bottle: 40, 10 and 8 respectively.

a What is the ratio?

Answer:

b Reduce this down to the lowest ratio.

Answer:

QUESTION 10

The ratio of energy in the nutritional information for a 2-litre orange juice bottle compared to a 2-litre diet soft drink bottle is 340 kJ to 3 kJ.

a What is the ratio of the two energy levels?

Answer:

b What is the lowest ratio you can reduce this to?

Answer:

Section A: Information Displayed in Tables

Information is often displayed in tables and charts for people to read to retrieve various bits of information. This is common in day-to-day activities such as timetables for buses and trains, viewing sales figures for different products or the results of a questionnaire.

In the hospitality industry, tables are often used to record sales figures, showing trends and highlighting particularly busy or quiet periods. Have a look at the table below and answer the questions that follow.

Total Expenditure	Week No.	Sales				Total Sales	Profit / Loss
		Bar	Bistro	Restaurant	Room Service		
£765	1	£196	£293	£581	£95	£1165	£400
£833	2	£231	£300	£675	£129	£1335	£502
£795	3	£210	£286	£615	£89	£1200	£405
£998	4	£287	£332	£704	£140	£1463	£465
£1225	5	£400	£376	£850	£160	£1786	£561

QUESTION 1

How many categories of sales are shown in the table?

_____

_____

QUESTION 2

In which week were Bistro sales at their lowest?

_____

_____

QUESTION 3

In how many weeks was expenditure over £800?

_____

_____

QUESTION 4

Does a rise in sales automatically result in a rise in profit?

_____

QUESTION 5

Which area generated the lowest sales?

_____

_____

Section B: Information Displayed in Charts

Similar to the use of tables, charts provide a graphical and simplified view of what can sometimes represent a large amount of information, also referred to as data.

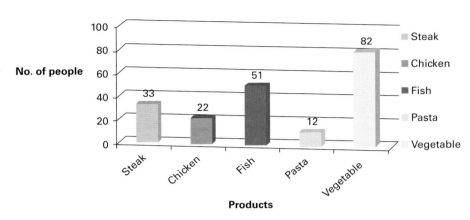

QUESTION 1

What does this graph show?

_____

_____

QUESTION 2

How many products are shown on the chart?

_____

QUESTION 3

Which product is the most popular with the consumers?

_____

QUESTION 4

Why would a hospitality business be interested in finding out the popularity of different products?

_____

_____

_____

_____

_____

Unit 18: Calculating Food Costs, Selling Prices and Making a Profit

The hospitality industry is largely made up of commercially focused businesses of various types (restaurants, hotels, bars, etc.) with the intention of making a profit so that they can survive (pay staff, suppliers and other bills) and make plans for the future.

In order to achieve this objective, it is essential to have an awareness of costs and how to calculate selling prices that will achieve enough profit to allow the business to meet its financial goals.

Section A: Costings

To determine a selling price of a recipe or a dish, the first task is to calculate its cost.

When making multiple portions of food and using ingredients in many different quantities, it is important to be able to calculate ingredient costs accurately. Look at the example below when making a génoise sponge.

Dish: Génoise sponge

Number of portions: 8

Ingredient	Quantity required	Unit of purchase	Unit cost	Recipe cost
Eggs (number)	4	30	£6.00	£0.80
Caster sugar (g)	100	1000	£2.50	£0.25
Soft flour (g)	100	1000	£1.20	£0.12
Butter (g)	50	1000	£4.00	£0.20
			Total cost	£1.37
			Cost per portion	£0.17

To calculate the recipe cost of this basic sponge, the unit cost has been divided by the unit of purchase (how the item is purchased) and multiplied by the amount required in the recipe.

EXAMPLE:

Taking the caster sugar example above, the unit cost is £2.50 for 1000g (1kg) and the amount required for the recipe is 100g. To calculate the amount used in the recipe, the following calculation is used.

£2.50 ÷ 1000 × 100 = £0.25

QUESTION 1

The costs for making 8 portions of génoise sponge are shown above. Now calculate the cost of making 12 portions of génoise sponge using the table on page 50.

Dish: Génoise sponge

Number of portions: 12

Ingredient	Quantity required	Unit of purchase	Unit cost	Recipe cost
Eggs (number)	6	24	£4.50	
Caster sugar (g)	150	500	£1.10	
Soft flour (g)	150	500	£0.90	
Butter (g)	75	250	£0.95	
			Total cost	
			Cost per portion	

Section B: Gross and Net Profit

Gross profit is a simple calculation that expresses the difference between the price that materials or goods (food) were bought for and the price at which they were sold.

EXAMPLE:

If the food costs to produce a dish come to £2.50 and the dish is sold for £7.50, the gross profit produced is £5.00.

Selling price (£7.50) – Food costs (£2.50) = Gross Profit (£5.00).

For budgeting and target setting purposes, it is common for gross profits to be expressed as percentages. To produce a percentage, the profit (£5.00) has to be expressed in terms of how much of the selling price (£7.50) it represents. To achieve this, the profit (£5.00) has to be divided by the selling price (£7.50) and then multiplied by 100.

£5.00 ÷ £7.50 × 100 = 66.66%

This shows that the £5.00 profit represents 66.66% or two-thirds (2/3) of the selling price at £7.50.

Net Profit

Net profit (or loss) expresses the difference between the price that materials or goods (food) were sold for with **all** associated costs subtracted. This includes the materials costs (e.g. food), labour costs and all other overhead costs (e.g. packaging, power costs, rent, etc.)

For example, if the selling price (sales) of a dinner for 100 people came to £1000.00, the food costs totalled £250.00, labour costs were £400.00 and associated overhead costs came to £150.00, the net profit would be £200.00.

Sales =	£1000.00
Food costs =	£250.00
Labour costs =	£400.00
Overheads =	£150.00
Total costs =	£800.00

Sales (£1000.00) – Total Costs (£800.00) = Net Profit (£200.00)

In the same way as for gross profits, net profits are also commonly expressed as percentages.

Net Profit (£200.00) divided by Sales (£1000.00) and multiplied by 100.

£200.00 ÷ £1000.00 × 100 = 20%

QUESTION 1

Express the gross profit (GP) in money (£) and as a percentage (%) in the table below.

Selling Price	Food Cost	Gross Profit (£)	GP as %
£10.00	£2.75		
£12.50	£4.30		
£7.95	£3.10		
£14.90	£4.65		
£31.65	£7.90		

QUESTION 2

Express the net profit (NP) in money (£) and as a percentage (%) in the table below.

Sales	Food Costs	Labour Costs	Overheads	Total Costs	Net Profit (£)	Net Profit as %
£140.55	£40.99	£50.50	£23.34			
£175.98	£55.45	£61.25	£34.00			
£268.94	£81.38	£90.45	£74.88			
£555.65	£120.00	£155.98	£111.54			
£1 010.80	£300.70	£240.54	£230.78			

Section C: Calculating the Selling Price

Price can be a sensitive issue. If priced too high, a dish may not sell or customers may complain or not return to the business as they may feel they have not received value for money. Alternately, if a dish is underpriced and does not make a profit, the business will be damaged financially and will face problems in the future if it does not rectify the situation.

A method to ensure that a profit margin is achieved is to build a target percentage of gross profit into the selling price. For example, if the food costs for a dish total £3.00 and a gross profit target is set at 70%, the food costs as a percentage of the selling price can only represent 30%. It is important to note that the selling price is the total amount of money that will be received so this has to represent 100% for the purpose of this calculation.

The two charts below show how this is broken down in percentage and monetary formats.

In basic terms, food costs + gross profit = selling price

To calculate the selling price on this basis, the food costs have to be expressed as a percentage of the selling price using the following calculation.

Food cost ÷ Food cost as a % of the selling price × 100

For example, if food costs for a dish come to £4.50 and the gross profit target is 75%, the food cost as a percentage of the targeted sale is 25%.

To calculate the selling price based on this information:

$$\frac{£4.50}{25} \times 100 = £18.00$$

By dividing £4.50 by 25, this brings the figure down to 1% of the selling price (£0.18). By then multiplying by 100, it brings the figure up to 100%, the selling price (£18.00). As long as you have the food cost and the target gross profit percentage, this is sufficient information to calculate the selling price.

To test the example above, divide £18.00 by 100 (to get 1%) and multiply by 25. The answer is £4.50 (food cost).

Doing the same in dividing £15.00 by 100 (to get 1%), this time multiplying by 75, the answer is £13.50 (gross profit).

£4.50 + £13.50 = £18.00 (selling price)

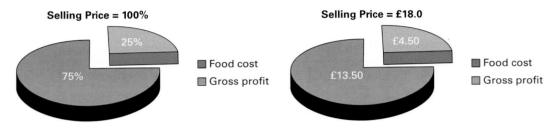

QUESTION 1

Calculate the selling price from the food cost and gross profit target indicated in the table below.

Food Costs	Gross Profit Target	Food Cost as % of Selling Price	Selling Price
£3.55	65%	35	
£4.65	70%	30	
£2.32	75%	25	
£5.00	80%	20	
£1.24	85%	15	

Unit 19:

Practice Written Exam for the Hospitality and Catering Industry

Reading time: 10 minutes

Writing time: 1 hour 30 minutes

Section A: Literacy

Section B: General Mathematics

Section C: Trade Mathematics

QUESTION and ANSWER BOOK

Section	Topic	Number of questions	Marks
A	Literacy	7	22
B	General Mathematics	11	26
C	Trade Mathematics	40	52
		Total 58	Total 100

The sections may be completed in the order of your choice.

NO CALCULATORS are to be used during the exam.

Spelling

Read the passage below, and then <u>underline</u> the 20 spelling errors.   10 marks

A conference centre emplyes eighteen staff. Twelfe of the staff work in
the kitchen. Friday and Saturday nights are often the busiest time for
functions. As preparartion begings for the Friday night function, two
staff members ring up to say that they are unwell and are unable to work.
Fortunatly, there are two other people who had aplied to work at the
centre that day, so they were asked to come in to work on a trial basis that
night.

An apprentice chef starts preparing the soup. All the ingrediants that are
needed for the soup had to be colected from the store. The storerom
was well stocked and it did not take long to retreve the ingredients.
Meenwhile, the other two cooks begin work on the enterees.

There are over 180 patrons atending the Friday night function and some
of the crokery needs to be replased as they have been chiped in the
dishwasher. One of the kitchenhands starts on this task and eventually
seventen plates are replaced. The other kitchenhand swepps up and
cleans around the kitchen before assisting with preparing the food.

Correct the spelling errors by writing them out with the correct spelling below:

_____

_____

Alphabetizing

Put the following words into alphabetical order.

6 marks

Clean cutlery	pak choi
Commis chef	Microwave oven
Food preparation	Soup
Entrée	Function centre
Flame grill	Braise
Dishwasher	Extra virgin olive oil

_____

_____

_____

_____

_____

_____

_____
_____
_____
_____
_____

Comprehension

Short-answer questions

Specific instructions to students

- Read the following activity and then answer the questions accordingly.

Read the following passage and answer the questions below.

350 guests were invited to a reception after a wedding. The wedding was delightful and everything went off without a hitch. Guests started to arrive at the reception venue at 6.00 p.m. and they all needed to be seated by 6.30 p.m.

The limousines arrived with the bridal party at 6.45 p.m. and everyone was ushered into the dining room The celebrant could not attend as he had to preside over a wake after a funeral. Everyone was looking forward to seeing the bride and groom as they had spent a lot of time getting photographed in the nearby gardens. Two staff made their way to the bridal table with Champagne for the newlyweds. Unfortunately, one waiter slipped and spilt Champagne all over the bride! The groom was shocked, but not as much as the bride. The waiters all worked feverishly to help the bride, who luckily saw the funny side of the incident.

As the guests remained seated, the waiters moved around the room delivering the entrées. The head chef came out and greeted the bridal party and said that he was preparing his finest dishes for them all. The kitchen staff then immediately set about cooking the dishes, but there was one problem; the gas was cut off due to an accident in which a delivery lorry had collided with the limousine. What could the chef do? Gas bottles were brought inside to use for the cooking, but everything went slowly. The waiters quickly shuffled between the tables, topping up the guests' drinks and keeping everyone merry. The entrées came out slowly, but at least they were cooked. The chef was highly apologetic and the bridal party left around 10.00 p.m. in a taxi. The damage to the limousine was too extensive and it needed to be towed away.
All the staff at the function centre breathed a sigh of relief and began to pack up.

QUESTION 1   1 mark

How many guests were there and at what time did they
need to be seated?

Answer:

_____

_____

QUESTION 2   1 mark

Why was the celebrant unable to come to the reception?

Answer:

_____

QUESTION 3   1 mark

Why was the groom 'shocked'?

Answer:

_____

_____

QUESTION 4   1 mark

Why was there a problem in the kitchen?

Answer:

_____

_____

_____

QUESTION 5   2 marks

How long was the bridal party at the reception for?

Answer:

_____

_____

_____

Section B: General Mathematics

QUESTION 1   1 + 1 + 1 = 3 marks

What unit of measurement would you use to measure:

a flour?

Answer:

_____

b oven temperature?

Answer:

_____

c cooking oil?

Answer:

_____

QUESTION 2   1 + 1 + 1 = 3 marks

For each of the following, give an example of where it may be found in the hospitality industry:

a percentages?

Answer:

_____

_____

_____

b decimals?

Answer:

_____

_____

c fractions?

Answer:

_____

_____

QUESTION 3   1 + 1 = 2 marks

Convert the following units:

a 3 kilograms to grams

Answer:

_____

b 500 grams to kilograms

Answer:

_____

QUESTION 4   2 marks

Write the following in descending order:

0.7   0.71   7.1   70.1   701.00   7.0

Answer:

_____

QUESTION 5   1 + 1 = 2 marks

Write the decimal number that is between the following:

a 0.1 and 0.2

Answer:

_____

b 1.3 and 1.4

Answer:

_____

QUESTION 6   1 + 1 = 2 marks

Round off the following numbers to two (2) decimal places:

a 5.177

Answer:

_____

b 12.655

Answer:

_____

QUESTION 7   1 + 1 = 2 marks

Estimate the following by approximation:

a 101×81

Answer:

_____

b 399×21

Answer:

_____

QUESTION 8   1 + 1 = 2 marks

What do the following add up to?

a £7, £13.57 and £163.99

Answer:

_____

b 4, 5.73 and 229.57

Answer:

QUESTION 9   1 + 1 = 2 marks

Subtract the following:

a 196 from 813

Answer:

---

b 5556 from 9223

Answer:

QUESTION 10   1 + 1 = 2 marks

Use division to solve:

a 4824 divided by 0.3

Answer:

---

b 84.2 ÷ 0.4

Answer:

QUESTION 11   2 + 2 = 4 marks

Using BODMAS solve:

a $(3 \times 7) \times 4 + 9 - 5$

Answer:

---

b $(8 \times 12) \times 2 + 8 - 4$

Answer:

Section C: Trade Mathematics

Basic operations

Addition

QUESTION 1   1 mark

A chef uses 65 mL, 118 mL, 235 mL and 450 mL of milk to make several different dishes in a kitchen. How much milk has been used in total?

Answer:

QUESTION 2   1 mark

A bistro charges £142 for meals and £68 for drinks. How much is the total bill?

Answer:

Subtraction

QUESTION 1   1 mark

A delivery vehicle is filled up with 36 litres of petrol. The tank is now at its maximum of 52 litres. The driver uses the following amounts of petrol on each day:

Monday – 5 litres

Tuesday – 11 litres

Wednesday – 10 litres

Thursday – 8 litres

Friday – 7 litres

How many litres of petrol are left in the tank?

Answer:

QUESTION 2   1 mark

A restaurant bill comes to £366.00. The customers have a voucher to deduct 10% from the bill. How much does the final bill come to?

Answer:

Multiplication

QUESTION 1   1 mark

A conference centre kitchen uses 3 kg of green pepper, 5 kg of red onions and 0.5 kg of cos lettuce when preparing a salad. How much of each ingredient, in kg, is needed if the same salad is made up 18 times?

Answer:

QUESTION 2   1 mark

If a chef uses 3 kg of flour each day for different preparations, how much would be used over a month with 31 days?

Answer:

Division

QUESTION 1   1 mark

A chef has 56 litres of pasta sauce. The pasta sauce is held in seven containers. How many litres are there in each container?

Answer:

QUESTION 2   1 mark

A conference centre has 488 new steak knives that are stored in 6 boxes. How many steak knives are there in each box?

Answer:

Decimals

Addition

QUESTION 1   1 + 1 = 2 marks

A set of knives are purchased for £46.99, and then a chopping board is also purchased for £24.50.

a How much will be paid in total?

Answer:

_____

b How much change is given from two £50 notes?

Answer:

_____

QUESTION 2   1 + 1 = 2 marks

A chef buys the following for her kitchen: 3kg of spaghetti for £6.99, 1 litre of pasta sauce for £2.95, 4 litres of olive oil for £19.99 and two ceramic dishes for £23.95.

a What is the total cost?

Answer:

_____

b How much change will she receive from three £20 notes?

Answer:

_____

Subtraction

QUESTION 1   1 + 1 = 2 marks

A chef in a bistro completes an order that is sold for £22.50, and then a discount of £4.50 is given.

a How much does the order cost after the discount?

Answer:

_____

b How much change will he need if £50 is paid?

Answer:

_____

QUESTION 2   1 mark

A commis chef uses 1.75 kg of flour from a 10 kg bag to make some cookies. How much flour is left?

Answer:

_____

Multiplication

QUESTION 1   1 mark

A chef buys 20 litres of extra virgin olive oil. If one litre costs £6.50, what is the total cost for 20 litres?

Answer:

_____

QUESTION 2   1 + 1 = 2 marks

A starter dish consists of three spring rolls. Each spring roll costs £1.80 to produce.

a How much does the dish cost to make

Answer:

_____

b How much change will be needed from £10.00 if it is sold at cost price?

Answer:

_____

Division

QUESTION 1   1 mark

An executive chef earns £990.50 over 5 days. How much does she earn per day?

Answer:

_____

QUESTION 2   1 mark

A restaurant bill totals £512.00 for 8 people. How much does each person pay if they split the bill evenly?

Answer:

_____

Fractions

QUESTION 1   1 mark

$\frac{2}{3} + \frac{3}{4} =$

Answer:

_____

QUESTION 2 — 1 mark

$\frac{4}{5} - \frac{1}{3} =$

Answer:

QUESTION 3 — 1 mark

$\frac{2}{3} \times \frac{1}{4} =$

Answer:

QUESTION 4 — 1 mark

$\frac{3}{4} \div \frac{1}{2} =$

Answer:

Percentages

QUESTION 1 — 1 mark

A set of electronic scales normally costs £90.00. A supplier is having a sale with 20% discount from the normal price. What is the discounted sale price?

Answer:

QUESTION 2 — 1 mark

A cutlery set is priced at £140 per set. A supplier offers a 20% discount for regular customers. What would the selling price be per set with the discount applied?

Answer:

Measurement

QUESTION 1 — 1 mark

How many millilitres are there in 3.85 litres?

Answer:

QUESTION 2 — 1 mark

2285 millilitres converts to how many litres?

Answer:

Circumference

QUESTION 1 — 1 mark

What is the circumference of a ice-cream machine with a diameter of 14 cm?

Answer:

QUESTION 2 — 1 mark

What is the circumference of a saucepan with a diameter of 30 cm?

Answer:

Diameter

QUESTION 1 — 1 mark

What is the diameter of a dinner plate with a circumference of 90 cm?

Answer:

QUESTION 2 — 1 mark

What is the diameter of a round table with a circumference of 280 cm?

Answer:

Area

QUESTION 1 — 1 mark

A bistro kitchen area is 4.5 m by 1.8 m. What is its total area?

Answer:

QUESTION 2 — 1 mark

If a function centre dining room measures 35 m $\times$ 30 m, what is its total area?

Answer:

Volume of a cube

QUESTION 1   1 mark

How many cubic metres are there in a storage area 15 m long by 5 m wide by 3m high?

Answer:

_____

QUESTION 2   1 mark

An apprentice chef uses a baking tray for lasagna with the following dimensions: 60 cm $\times$ 15 cm $\times$ 10 cm. How many cubic centimetres of space is available on the tray?

Answer:

_____

Volume of a cylinder

QUESTION 1   2 marks

A container used for storing flour has a radius of 8 cm and a height of 30 cm. What volume can it hold?

Answer:

_____

QUESTION 2   2 marks

A container for storing dried fruit has a radius of 5 cm and a height of 28 cm. What volume can it hold?

Answer:

_____

Earning wages

QUESTION 1   2 marks

A commis chef earns £245.50 net (after tax) per week. How much does he earn per year? (Note that there are 52 weeks in a year.)

Answer:

_____

QUESTION 2   2 marks

If a bistro chef earns £2 per hour, how much would she earn for a 35-hour week?

Answer:

_____

Squaring numbers

QUESTION 1   2 marks

What is 11 squared?

Answer:

_____

QUESTION 2   2 marks

A dining room area in a restaurant measures 12.2 $\times$ 12.2 metres. What is the total area?

Answer:

_____

Ratio

QUESTION 1   2 marks

A 2-litre bottle of cordial is made up of 25% fruit juice and 75% of a mixture of water, reconstituted apple juice and various flavours and additives. What is the lowest ratio of fruit juice to mixture?

Answer:

_____

QUESTION 2   2 marks

A tropical fruit juice mixture contains 40% orange juice, 25% mango juice, 20% pineapple juice and the rest is water.

a What percentage is made up of water?

Answer:

_____

b What percentage of the mixture do the juices make up?

Answer:

_____

Hospitality and Catering Glossary

Barista This term is of Italian origin and refers to someone who has acquired some level of expertise in the preparation of espresso-based coffee

Bistro cook A cook who works at a small restaurant, club or hotel. A bistro cook may tend to cook slow-cooked foods like braised meats

Braise Cooking method where food (usually meat) is first browned in oil and then cooked slowly in a liquid (wine, stock or water)

Canapé A base of bread, pastry or porcelain onto which savoury food is placed as a pre-dinner snack or as a course at the end of a meal prior to dessert

Chef de cuisine Similar to an executive chef. A French term that traditionally means head chef at a location

Commis chef This is the apprentice in larger kitchens who works under the other chefs to gain experience and knowledge

Defrost To slowly increase the temperature of a freezer, fridge or food portion so as to thaw it out and remove the ice

Deep fry The process of cooking food by immersion in hot fat or oil in a deep pan or electric fryer to give a crisp, golden coating.

Deep fryer A gas or electrical device that is used for cooking or deep frying food

Dessert A course that typically comes at the end of the meal

En croute (French) Cooked in pastry e.g. Beef Wellington

Entrée A French term meaning a savoury course served at the beginning of a meal service

Escalope (French) Refers to a thinly sliced, boneless round cut of meat that is batted until thin

Flan An open pastry tart with a filling that can be sweet (e.g. lemon, fruit) or savoury (e.g. quiche)

Gourmet (French) Food connoisseur

Main course The featured or primary dish in a meal

Marinade A mixture of wet or dry ingredients used to flavour or tenderize a food prior to cooking

Nutrients The essential parts of food that are vital for health

Pâté (French) 'Paste'.1. Pâté refers to either a smooth or coarse product made from meat, poultry, fish, vegetable, offal or game that has been blended and cooked with cream, butter and eggs. 2. Pâté is different base pastry products, sweet, short, lining, puff, choux

Purée (French) A smooth paste of a particular ingredient or a soup that is passed through a sieve

Ramekin Individual or small ceramic round baking dish

Roast To cook food in an oven or on a spit over a fire with the aid of fat

Sous chef The direct assistant to the chef de cuisine, who can be considered second in charge

Steam The cooking of food in steam, over rapidly boiling water or other liquid. The food is usually suspended above such liquid by means of a trivet or steaming basket, although in the case of puddings, the basin actually sits in the water.

Stock A cooked flavoured liquid that is used as a cooking liquor or base for a sauce

Whisk To beat air into a mixture until it is soft

Maths and English Glossary

Adjectives   Describes things, people and places, such as 'sharp', 'warm' or 'handsome'

Adverbs   Describes the way something happens, such as 'slowly', 'often' or 'quickly'

Homophones   Words that sound the same, but are spelt differently and have different meanings

Imperial   A system of units for measurements e.g. pounds and inches

Metric   An international system of units for measurement. This is a decimal system of units based on the metre as a unit length and the kilogram as a unit mass

Nouns   Names of things, people and places, such as 'chair', 'George' or 'Sheffield'

Pronouns   Short words like 'it', 'you', 'we' or 'they', etc. used instead of actual names

Ratio   A way to compare the amounts of something

Verbs   Words to describe what you are 'doing', such as 'to mix', 'smile/frown' or 'walking'

Formulae and Data

Circumference of a Circle

$C = \pi \times d$
where: C = circumference, π = 3.14, d = diameter

Diameter of a Circle

Diameter (d) of a circle $= \dfrac{\text{circumference}}{\pi\,(3.14)}$

Area

Area = length $\times$ breadth and is given in square units
    $= l \times b$

Volume of a Cube

Volume of a cube = length $\times$ width $\times$ height and is given in cubic units
    $= l \times w \times h$

Volume of a Cylinder

Volume of cylinder (V_c) $= \pi\,(3.14) \times r^2\,(\text{radius} \times \text{radius}) \times \text{height}$
    $V_c = \pi \times r^2 \times h$

Times Tables

1

1 × 1 = 1
2 × 1 = 2
3 × 1 = 3
4 × 1 = 4
5 × 1 = 5
6 × 1 = 6
7 × 1 = 7
8 × 1 = 8
9 × 1 = 9
10 × 1 = 10
11 × 1 = 11
12 × 1 = 12

2

1 × 2 = 2
2 × 2 = 4
3 × 2 = 6
4 × 2 = 8
5 × 2 = 10
6 × 2 = 12
7 × 2 = 14
8 × 2 = 16
9 × 2 = 18
10 × 2 = 20
11 × 2 = 22
12 × 2 = 24

3

1 × 3 = 3
2 × 3 = 6
3 × 3 = 9
4 × 3 = 12
5 × 3 = 15
6 × 3 = 18
7 × 3 = 21
8 × 3 = 24
9 × 3 = 27
10 × 3 = 30
11 × 3 = 33
12 × 3 = 36

4

1 × 4 = 4
2 × 4 = 8
3 × 4 = 12
4 × 4 = 16
5 × 4 = 20
6 × 4 = 24
7 × 4 = 28
8 × 4 = 32
9 × 4 = 36
10 × 4 = 40
11 × 4 = 44
12 × 4 = 48

5

1 × 5 = 5
2 × 5 = 10
3 × 5 = 15
4 × 5 = 20
5 × 5 = 25
6 × 5 = 30
7 × 5 = 35
8 × 5 = 40
9 × 5 = 45
10 × 5 = 50
11 × 5 = 55
12 × 5 = 60

6

1 × 6 = 6
2 × 6 = 12
3 × 6 = 18
4 × 6 = 24
5 × 6 = 30
6 × 6 = 36
7 × 6 = 42
8 × 6 = 48
9 × 6 = 54
10 × 6 = 60
11 × 6 = 66
12 × 6 = 72

7

1 × 7 = 7
2 × 7 = 14
3 × 7 = 21
4 × 7 = 28
5 × 7 = 35
6 × 7 = 42
7 × 7 = 49
8 × 7 = 56
9 × 7 = 63
10 × 7 = 70
11 × 7 = 77
12 × 7 = 84

8

1 × 8 = 8
2 × 8 = 16
3 × 8 = 24
4 × 8 = 32
5 × 8 = 40
6 × 8 = 48
7 × 8 = 56
8 × 8 = 64
9 × 8 = 72
10 × 8 = 80
11 × 8 = 88
12 × 8 = 96

9

1 × 9 = 9
2 × 9 = 18
3 × 9 = 27
4 × 9 = 36
5 × 9 = 45
6 × 9 = 54
7 × 9 = 63
8 × 9 = 72
9 × 9 = 81
10 × 9 = 90
11 × 9 = 99
12 × 9 = 108

10

1 × 10 = 10
2 × 10 = 20
3 × 10 = 30
4 × 10 = 40
5 × 10 = 50
6 × 10 = 60
7 × 10 = 70
8 × 10 = 80
9 × 10 = 90
10 × 10 = 100
11 × 10 = 110
12 × 10 = 120

11

1 × 11 = 11
2 × 11 = 22
3 × 11 = 33
4 × 11 = 44
5 × 11 = 55
6 × 11 = 66
7 × 11 = 77
8 × 11 = 88
9 × 11 = 99
10 × 11 = 110
11 × 11 = 121
12 × 11 = 132

12

1 × 12 = 12
2 × 12 = 24
3 × 12 = 36
4 × 12 = 48
5 × 12 = 60
6 × 12 = 72
7 × 12 = 84
8 × 12 = 96
9 × 12 = 108
10 × 12 = 120
11 × 12 = 132
12 × 12 = 144

Multiplication Grid

×	1	2	3	4	5	6	7	8	9	10	11	12
1	1	2	3	4	5	6	7	8	9	10	11	12
2	2	4	6	8	10	12	14	16	18	20	22	24
3	3	6	9	12	15	18	21	24	27	30	33	36
4	4	8	12	16	20	24	28	32	36	40	44	48
5	5	10	15	20	25	30	35	40	45	50	55	60
6	6	12	18	24	30	36	42	48	54	60	66	72
7	7	14	21	28	35	42	49	56	63	70	77	84
8	8	16	24	32	40	48	56	64	72	80	88	96
9	9	18	27	36	45	54	63	72	81	90	99	108
10	10	20	30	40	50	60	70	80	90	100	110	120
11	11	22	33	44	55	66	77	88	99	110	121	132
12	12	24	36	48	60	72	84	96	108	120	132	144

Maths and English for Hospitality and Catering

Online Answer Guide

To access the Answer Guide for Maths and English for Hospitality and Catering follow these simple steps:

1) Copy the following link into your web browser:

http://www.cengagebrain.co.uk/shop/isbn/9781408072691

2) Click on the Free Study Tools Link.

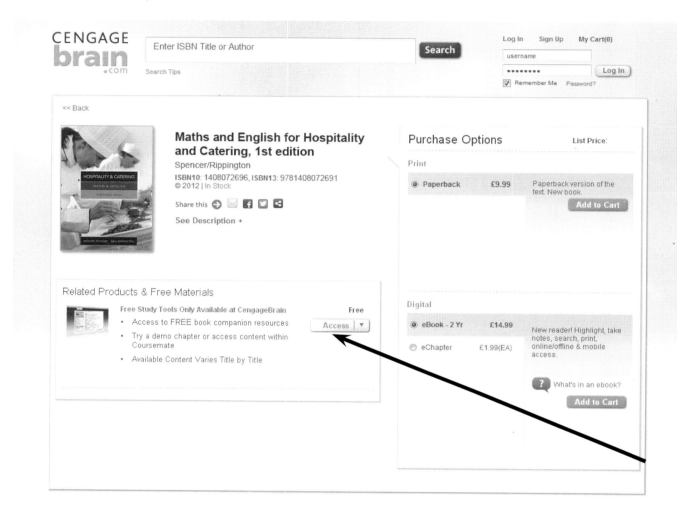

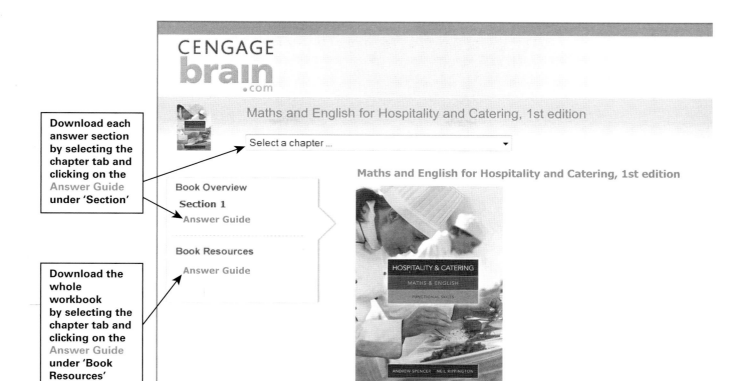

Download each answer section by selecting the chapter tab and clicking on the Answer Guide under 'Section'

Download the whole workbook by selecting the chapter tab and clicking on the Answer Guide under 'Book Resources'

Notes

Notes

Notes

Notes

Notes